Egypt

HOWARD GUTNER

Children's Press®
An Imprint of Scholastic Inc.
New York Toronto London Auckland Sydney
Mexico City New Delhi Hong Kong
Danbury, Connecticut

Library of Congress Cataloging-in-Publication Data

Gutner, Howard, 1954–
  Egypt / by Howard Gutner.
    p. cm. — (A true book)
  Includes index.
    ISBN-13: 978-0-531-16889-9 (lib. bdg.)   978-0-531-21356-8 (pbk.)
    ISBN-10: 0-531-16889-1 (lib. bdg.)   0-531-21356-0 (pbk.)
  1. Egypt—Juvenile literature. I. Title. II. Series.

DT49.G88 2009
962—dc22   2008014784

Produced by Weldon Owen Education Inc.

1 2 3 4 5 6 7 8 9 10 R 18 17 16 15 14 13 12 11 10 09

Find the Truth!

Everything you are about to read is true *except* for one of the sentences on this page.

Which one is **TRUE**?

T or F   The addax antelope spends the day searching for food in the desert.

T or F   The source of the Sphinx's broken nose is a mystery.

Find the answers in this book.

Contents

THE **BIG** TRUTH!

Life After Life

Mummy

Ancient Egyptians worshipped hundreds of gods.

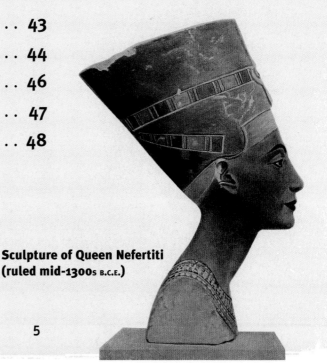

Sculpture of Queen Nefertiti
(ruled mid-1300s B.C.E.)

The Great Pyramid of Giza is near the city of Cairo. It was built as a tomb about 4,500 years ago. It is made out of more than 2,000,000 blocks of stone. Each block weighs an average of 2.5 tons.

CHAPTER 1

Marvelous Things

Each year, about 11 million people come from all over the world to visit Egypt. They travel to Egypt for the same reason a Greek historian went there about 2,500 years ago. After his trip, Herodotus (hih-RAHD-uh-tuhs) wrote, "Nowhere are there so many marvelous things."

The Great Pyramid is taller than a 45-story skyscraper.

Egypt

The temple of Karnak complex is near the city of Luxor. The symbols, or hieroglyphs, on the temple give information about life in ancient times.

Egyptian hieroglyphic writing used a combination of pictures to make a word.

Egypt has one of the longest histories of any country on Earth. About 5,000 years ago, Egyptians built one of the world's earliest civilizations. They were among the first people to invent a written language. They were also among the first to make great buildings out of stone. Amazingly, many of these structures are still standing.

Throughout Egypt, there are reminders of its glorious past. People all over the country, however, are working hard to make sure Egypt has a glorious future as well. In recent years, the government has been working to improve its economy. It is trying to **irrigate** new farmland and build more towns to reduce overcrowding.

Every day, about half of Cairo's population crosses the Nile River using the 6th of October Bridge. The 6th of October was the starting date of the Arab-Israeli War of 1973.

In early spring, a fast, hot wind sometimes blows across the Egyptian desert. The wind picks up sand and often carries it into areas where people live. Winds move as quickly as 87 miles (140 kilometers) per hour and last for days. People stay inside their houses to keep safe.

CHAPTER 2

Land of Sand

Almost all of Egypt is desert. The Sahara Desert stretches east to west across the country. Only the hardiest plants and animals can survive there. Luckily, Egypt also has one of the world's longest rivers. Most Egyptians live in cities and villages close to the Nile River.

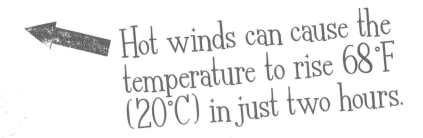

Hot winds can cause the temperature to rise 68°F (20°C) in just two hours.

Egypt and Its Neighbors

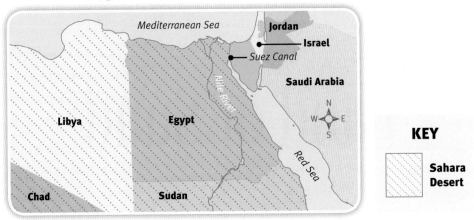

Animal Life

Temperatures in the Sahara Desert can top 110 °F (43 °C). But the vast area of dry sand is not as empty as it may look. Tough plants that can survive with very little water grow in some areas. Some kinds of snakes, lizards, and scorpions also live here.

Life is very different close to the Nile. The river provides water for crops and animals. There are many animals, including Nile crocodiles. The crocodiles eat fish and turtles and may even go after animals as large as hippos.

Amazing Addax

An antelope called an addax is well suited to the Sahara. It can go a month without drinking. It can survive on dew and water found in the grasses that it eats. Addaxes move around during the night when the temperature is cooler and rest during the day. Today, this species is endangered. There are fewer than 500 addaxes left in the wild.

In many farms throughout Egypt, children help their families by working in the fields.

Farming the Land

Farming is a key part of the Egyptian economy. Farmers who own small family farms are called *fellahin* (FELL-ah-heen) in Arabic. Fellahin grow crops that their families can eat, such as vegetables. They also grow crops, such as sugarcane and oranges, to sell in local markets.

In contrast, some huge farms in Egypt use paid labor and modern farm equipment. These farms lie near the mouth of the Nile River. Some of them are owned and run by the government. Others are owned and run by wealthy landowners. Most of the crops from these large farms, such as cotton and citrus fruit, are **exported**.

The fluffy white pods of the cotton plant are picked. The white fiber is spun into yarn, which is used to make fabric.

15

Other Income

Egypt straddles two continents, Asia and Africa. Each year, thousands of ships use Egypt's Suez Canal to pass between the continents. Egypt collects billions of dollars in tolls from the canal. It was not always a moneymaker for Egypt, however. At various times, the French and the British had some control over the canal and profited from it. In 1956, the Egyptians seized the waterway and won control over it.

Egypt has other sources of income as well. The economy gets a big boost from millions of tourists who come each year to look at Egypt's ancient treasures. In addition, Egypt makes money from natural gas and oil exports. Cotton, iron, and steel are important exports as well.

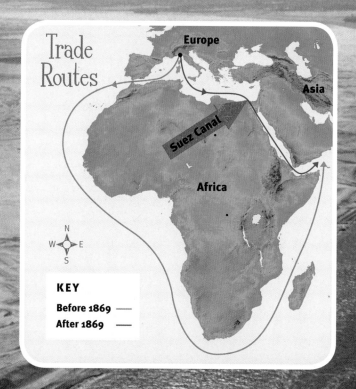

Trade Routes

Europe

Asia

Suez Canal

Africa

N
W · E
S

KEY

Before 1869 ——
After 1869 ——

The Suez Canal has been an important trade route since it was opened in 1869.

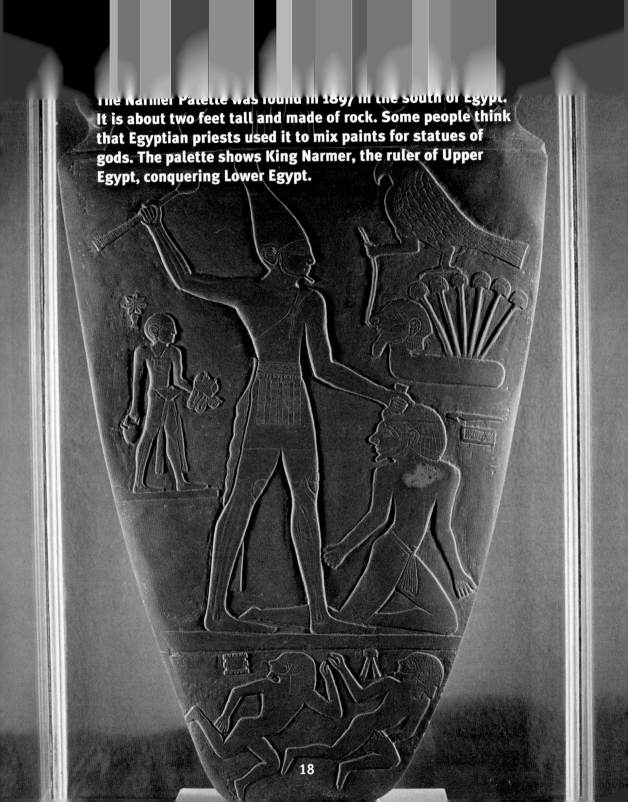

The Narmer Palette was found in 1897 in the south of Egypt. It is about two feet tall and made of rock. Some people think that Egyptian priests used it to mix paints for statues of gods. The palette shows King Narmer, the ruler of Upper Egypt, conquering Lower Egypt.

CHAPTER 3

An Ancient Land

People began to form small villages along the banks of the Nile River thousands of years ago. About 3,000 B.C.E., King Narmer united the villages to form Egypt. Since then, Egypt has been conquered and ruled by many other civilizations. The Greeks, Romans, Arabs, French, British, and other cultures have all influenced Egyptian life.

The Narmer Palette is still in excellent condition even though it is about 5,000 years old.

Egyptian Kings

Over time, kings in ancient Egypt became known as pharaohs. Pharaohs had absolute power. They made the laws, controlled the **resources**, and commanded the armies. They were even head priests.

Many pharaohs created ambitious art and architecture projects. They built temples to the gods. Pharaohs also built pyramids and other tombs to preserve their **mummified** bodies. Egyptians believed that bodies needed to be prepared for the life that occurred after death.

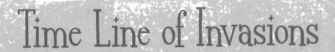

Time Line of Invasions

639 C.E. ➡️ **1517**

Arab armies invade Egypt. The new rulers introduce the religion of Islam.

Ottomans invade. They take over Egypt but don't tightly control it.

A New Republic

Conquerors brought new religions and languages to Egypt. Christianity arrived under Roman rule, around 40 C.E. Several hundred years later, invaders from the Arabian Peninsula brought Islam and the Arabic language to Egypt.

The last foreign ruling power, Great Britain, left Egypt in 1922. The British left Egypt with a king and a parliament in the style of the British political system.

1801 ➡

Ottoman army officer Muhammad Ali helps drive out the French, who invaded in 1798. He seizes power and later becomes Egypt's ruler.

➡ 1882

The British government orders thousands of troops into Egypt and takes control.

Improving the Nation

In 1952, a group of Egyptian military officers overthrew the king. A colonel named Gamal Abdel Nasser became president of Egypt in 1956. Nasser helped the poor to get land and a higher standard of living. He built the Aswan High Dam, which produces a huge amount of electricity and helps Egypt control its water supply.

Satellite Photo of Aswan High Dam

Nile River

Aswan High Dam

Lake Nasser

The Aswan High Dam has both helped and hurt farmers. The dam collects water for crops. However, it prevents flooding of the Nile, which carried rich, damp soil onto the riverbanks.

War and Peace

Egypt struggled with a new neighbor, Israel. Arab and Israeli leaders had disputes over land. Israel and Egypt went to war with each other and Egypt lost some of its land.

When Nasser died in 1970, the next president was Anwar Sadat. Sadat made some changes. He tried to open Egypt's economy to foreign **investors**. In 1979, Sadat signed a peace treaty with Israel. The treaty won Egypt back some land it had lost, but it angered some Arab leaders. Sadat was shot in 1981 by Arabs who were against his **policies**.

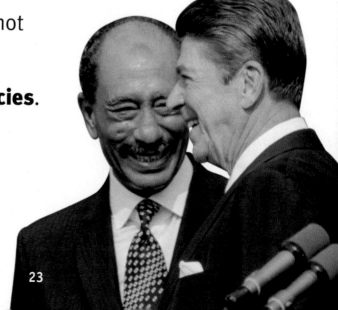

Anwar Sadat wanted closer ties with the United States. Here he is seen with former U.S. president Ronald Reagan.

Today's Government

After Sadat's death, Vice President Hosni Mubarak became president. Mubarak has stayed friendly with the United States. Many U.S. companies do business with Egypt. Mubarak has not given his citizens much political power, however. He declared a "state of emergency" in 1981 and has kept it in force ever since. This means he has the power to use the police and the military to stop any person or group he feels is dangerous.

In 2005, Hosni Mubarak began serving his fifth term as Egyptian president.

24

In 2005, the resort town Sharm El-Sheikh suffered from a series of terrorist attacks. Many Egyptians and non-Egyptians were killed.

Under Mubarak, people who want a different form of government don't have many options. Some groups have carried out terrorist attacks. They wanted to hurt Egypt's economy by scaring away tourists. Some people hoped that the attacks would force Mubarak out of office. How Mubarak and the rest of Egypt respond to this threat remains one of the country's greatest challenges.

Life After Life

Step One

The judge Anubis led the dead person's spirit to the scales of justice. The heart was weighed against a feather. Heavy hearts were said to be loaded down with bad deeds.

Step Two

Anubis threw heavy hearts to Ammit. The monster Ammit was known as Devourer of the Dead. The spirits with heavy hearts didn't go on to the afterlife.

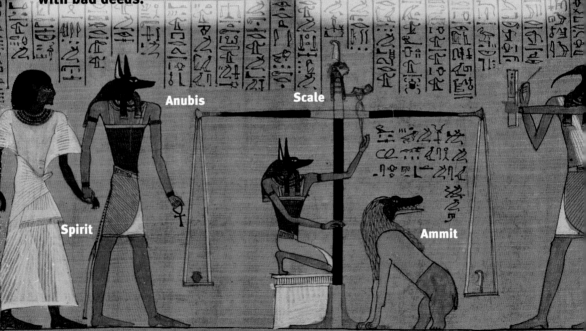

Anubis

Scale

Spirit

Ammit

What kind of painting is right for a tomb? Ancient Egyptians believed that death was just a short break before eternal life began. Bodies were made into mummies and placed inside tombs. Paintings inside some tombs showed how a person might travel to the next life.

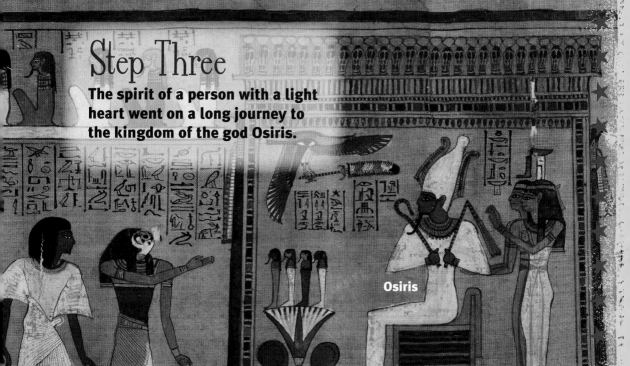

Step Three

The spirit of a person with a light heart went on a long journey to the kingdom of the god Osiris.

Osiris

The mask of the pharaoh Tutankhamun is made of gold and precious stones. It was found in his tomb, along with many other treasures.

CHAPTER 4

From Mummies to Movies

Ancient Egyptian art is still admired by people today. Art and mummies can be seen in major museums around the globe. Most ancient Egyptian art was made for the pharaohs or for temples that honored the gods. Today, the tradition of great art continues in modern art, music, dance, films, and literature.

Tutankhamun is known as the boy king. He ruled from about age 9 to when he died at about age 18.

Ancient Achievements

Imagine building a giant structure that would last more than 4,000 years. Now imagine building it at a time when there was very little construction equipment. Egyptians had to invent simple machines, such as ramps and levers. Pyramid architects measured millions of stone blocks, so that each would fit perfectly. The pyramids of Giza have remained strong for 4,500 years!

The thick stone walls of the pyramids of Giza were built to keep out people but to let in spirits. However, even in the time of the pharaohs, robbers broke in to steal treasures.

The Great Sphinx is near the Pyramids of Giza. They were built at about the same time. The Sphinx's head and body are carved out of a giant rock. Its legs and paws are made from stone blocks. It has a human face and the body of a lion. The monument stands about 66 feet (20 meters) high.

Nobody knows what happened to the Great Sphinx's nose.

Youssef Chahine

Egyptian director Youssef Chahine made 44 films during his career. He was known as the grand master of Arab cinema.

Hollywood in the East

Egypt has been called the Hollywood of the Arab world. Egyptians have been making films for more than 100 years. Some movies were made for Egyptian audiences; others were made for international audiences. Egyptian comedies, action movies, and dramas are popular all over the Arabic-speaking world.

Modern Art

Once the pharaohs ordered special works of art to be made. Today the Egyptian government encourages fine art exhibitions and competitions.

The Museum of Modern Egyptian Art in Cairo shows the work of modern Egyptian artists. Egypt also has a school of fine arts and a weaving school. Some of the weaving school's **tapestries** hang in museums around the world.

Egypt's well-known weaving school is named after its founder, Ramses Wissa Wassef. Animals and landscapes are often featured in the tapestries. Each may take months to complete.

33

Classical and Pop

Music is everywhere in Egypt. In large cities, street musicians play stringed instruments. Some folk musicians use instruments and rhythms similar to those used in ancient Egyptian music.

Popular Egyptian music is often based on classical Egyptian styles. Some musicians combine styles such as hip-hop and reggae with more traditional sounds. With computers and cable, many Egyptians also listen to Western music.

Angham Mohammad Ali Suleiman is one of Egypt's best-selling artists. She sings pop, jazz, and Arabic classical songs.

Art of the Written Word

In addition to creating one of the first written alphabets, Egyptians are also often credited with inventing books! The ancient Alexandrian Library once contained about 500,000 **scrolls**. Scholars came from all over the world to study there. Today, Alexandria has a modern library with space for eight million books.

The modern library in Alexandria has a high wall. It is engraved with letters from many different alphabets.

Bedouins (BEH-doo-ihnz) are a people who often travel with their animals to find grazing land. Bedouins herd small flocks of sheep, goats, or camels.

CHAPTER 5

Live Like an Egyptian

If you travel across Egypt, you'll hear different languages and come across various traditions and peoples. Arabic is the official language, though many people also speak English and French. Most Egyptians **descend** from both Ancient Egyptians and invaders from the Arabian Peninsula who settled in the area.

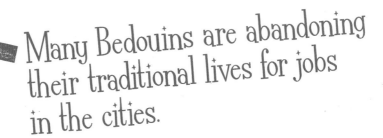

Many Bedouins are abandoning their traditional lives for jobs in the cities.

Daily Prayer

Most Egyptians are Muslims, or followers of the religion of Islam. Muslims believe in one god, whom they call Allah. Five times each day all over Egypt, a chosen person climbs to the top of a **mosque** and calls out "*Allah o Akbar.*" This means "God is great." Then Muslims know it is time to pray.

About 10 percent of Egyptians are Christians. Most belong to the Coptic Church.

The Abu al-Abbas al-Mursi mosque in Alexandria was constructed in 1307. It was later enlarged and altered. It has been restored many times.

Ramadan

Ramadan is an Islamic holy month. It takes place in the ninth month of the Islamic calendar. At this time, Muslims **fast** while the sun is up. At sunset, they hear a prayer call from a mosque, or on the radio or television. This means they can break the fast and eat supper. Normally, young children do not fast during Ramadan. Children often celebrate Ramadan with a lantern called a *fanoos*. These lanterns are usually made of colorful glass or plastic and tin.

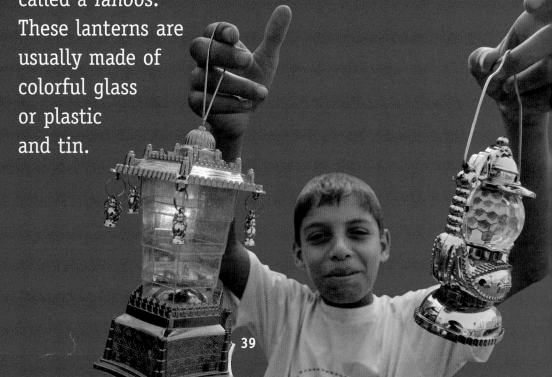

Growing Up

Egyptian children play many sports and games, but soccer is the most popular. Tennis, squash, basketball, and handball are also played often.

Children are usually required to attend school for about six to eight years. However, some children don't go to school. They drop out to help their families earn money.

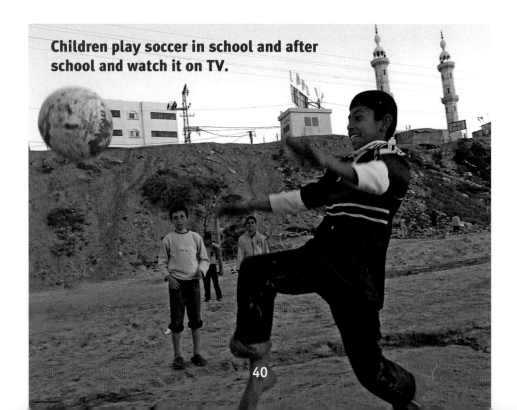

Children play soccer in school and after school and watch it on TV.

Egyptian Food

Egyptian cities have their own form of fast food. One popular option is *shawarma* (SHWAR-muh), thin slices of spicy meat and vegetables with flatbread. The bread is rolled up to form a sandwich.

The best-known Egyptian dish is called *ful medames*. It is made of seasoned fava beans and onions. Egyptians have eaten this dish for more than a thousand years.

Shawarma

To make a shawarma, slices of meat are shaved from a rotating skewer of chicken, lamb, beef, or other meat.

As Cairo grows, the space between the pyramids and the city gets smaller.

Past, Present, and Future

In some of Egypt's small villages, life seems to have changed little from the days of the pharaohs. However, life in cities, such as Cairo, is a mix of the old and the new.

Tall skyscrapers soar near stone buildings that are hundreds of years old. People can shop in traditional markets called souks or in bright new stores. Egypt's long, rich past remains alive as the country moves into the future. ★

True Statistics

Official name: The Arab Republic of Egypt

Size: 386,662 sq. mi. (1,001,449 sq. km). It's about three times the size of the state of New Mexico.

Currency: Egyptian pound

Population: About 80 million

Percentage of the population that can read and write: About 70 percent

Average age: 24.5 years

Percentage of Egyptians living along the Nile River and Suez Canal: About 99 percent

Did you find the truth?

F The addax antelope spends the day searching for food in the desert.

T The source of the Sphinx's broken nose is a mystery.

43

Resources

Books

Habeeb, William Mark. *Egypt* (Africa: Continent in the Balance). Broomall, PA: Mason Crest Publishers, 2007.

Heinrichs, Ann. *Egypt* (Enchantment of the World). New York: Children's Press, 2006.

Hobbs, Joseph J. *Egypt* (Modern World Nations). Philadelphia: Chelsea House Publishers, 2003.

Parker, Lewis K. *Egypt* (Discovering Cultures). New York: Benchmark Books/Marshall Cavendish, 2003.

Pateman, Robert, and Salwa El-Hamamsy. *Egypt* (Cultures of the World). New York: Benchmark Books/Marshall Cavendish, 2004.

Streissguth, Tom. *Egypt* (Country Explorers). Minneapolis, MN: Lerner Publications, 2008.

Strom, Laura Layton. *The Egyptian Science Gazette* (Shockwave: Science). New York: Children's Press, 2007.

Strom, Laura Layton. *Tombs and Treasure* (Shockwave: Social Studies). New York: Children's Press, 2007.

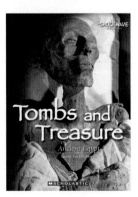

Organizations and Web Sites

The Cleveland Museum of Art
www.clemusart.com/kids/egypt/index.html
Find out more about ancient Egypt with fun games and activities.

Time for Kids
www.timeforkids.com/TFK/hh/goplaces/
main/0,20344,535892,00.html
Explore Egypt's land, history, and everyday life.

Places to Visit

The Metropolitan Museum of Art
1000 Fifth Avenue
New York, NY 10028-0198
(212) 535 7710
www.metmuseum.org
See a fine collection of ancient Egyptian art, with almost 36,000 objects.

The Rosicrucian Egyptian Museum & Planetarium
1664 Park Avenue
San Jose, CA 95191
(408) 947 3636
www.egyptianmuseum.org
Explore Ancient Egypt's view of the afterlife and a huge collection of human and animal mummies.

Important Words

descend – to belong to a later generation of a family

export – to send products to another country

fast – to go for a long time without eating

investor – someone who gives money with the belief that he or she will get back more money in the future

irrigate – to supply plants with water by artificial means, such as channels

mosque (MOSK) – a building used by Muslims for worship

mummify – to preserve a dead body so that it doesn't decay; ancient Egyptians mummified bodies by adding special salts and resins and wrapping them in cloth.

policy – a plan or principle that people use to guide them in making decisions or taking action

resource – a stock of materials or assets; natural resources of a country include oil, gas, timber, and minerals.

scroll – a document that is rolled up into the shape of a tube

tapestry – a fabric with designs woven into it or embroidered onto it

Index

Page numbers in **bold** indicate illustrations

About the Author

Howard Gutner has a degree in journalism from the University of Illinois and has written books about the *Titanic* and the Great Chicago Fire, as well as historical fiction. He makes his home in Brooklyn, New York.